my stars

are the ocean

LUNAIRIS

author of
Wildflowers In Bloom
Dreaming In Purple

Disclaimer:

All writing contained in this book is intellectual property of the author and exists in original written and electronic form. Writing, formatting, cover design, and editing is entirely by the author. Any third-party image licenses have been purchased by the author.

Registered copyright certificate has been obtained by the author under the Canadian Intellectual Property Office.

No portion of this book may be reproduced or recreated in any form without prior written permission from the author.

"LUNAIRIS " is a pseudonym used by Leanna Hewitt and is reserved as such.

The writing contained in this book is an exaggeration of reality inspired by the author's own emotions, memories, dreams, and life experiences. Any relatable emotions brought forth in the reader are purely coincidental and are not the responsibility of the author.

! Trigger warning: content describes sensitive events regarding mental health, abuse, loss, and vivid descriptions. May trigger relatable emotions. Please practice healthy self-care before, during, and after reading.

18+ Mature content warning: some of the content in this book may not be appropriate for young readers. Discretion is advised.

For more writing by LUNAIRIS,
follow @lunairispoetry on Instagram.

ISBN: 978-1-9994921-1-3

my stars

are the ocean

once upon a lifetime
I gazed upon the skies
galaxies fell into my eyes
in every moment
that I cried
my stars
became the ocean

the skies above

the seas below

my stars

are the ocean

the skies above

if you feel like
you are falling
ignite and ascend higher
into the cosmos
of yourself

WHAT STARS FEAR

I wonder often
if the stars fear the rising sun
knowing that their beauty
is only seen during the night
but they are always there
still existing, only hidden
by the day's light

I wonder if we fear
the darkness just the same
that once the sun sets
our light disappears
but it is always there
still existing, only hidden
by the shadow of night

*the stars still exist
so do you, my dear
even in the dark
and the light*

COUNT YOUR STARS

be thankful
for every star
in your sky
they are lighting
the dark spaces
of your life

MY UNIVERSE

my happy place
peace of my soul
my quiet and calm
the beating of my heart
my hopes and dreams
light of my life
my entire universe
will always be
my daughter

to the moon and beyond

STARKISSED SONNET

I wonder if ever, my soul will embrace forever
with the bittersweet taste of his flaming kiss
burning still, on my lips, until time does sever
memories of his goddess reminisced

will I trickle with starlight into love's gaze?
skies falling around us entwining by light
will he guide my cold feet against deep haze?
lead me to euphoria under full moon's night

I am but a collapsing star on erratic course
awaiting a disastrous moment to explode
surely an impact of soul's cosmic force
would spark a supernova, aching to behold

within me I carry a catastrophic universe
collide with my soul, force time's reverse

COLLISION COURSE

my stars were never meant
to align with yours
we are of opposites
that should never
have touched
you, the sun
I, the moon
though we did
defiant to the universe
we placed reality out of orbit
and destroyed everything
in our wake

Moondust

tonight
I saw you pull the moon
from the sky for me
my hope – even brighter
than the stars
then slowly
I saw it turning black
crumbling to dust
in your hands
through your fingers
and that
is why I cannot
pour my light
into your dark heart
ever again

Vortex

you must believe
the galaxies conspired
to revolve around your bones
I hate to disappoint you
my dear
see the bigger picture
you are a black hole
drawing in the light
around you
swallowing it whole
and I am the supernova
that will emerge from you
tenfold

TRAVEL

one day
I will travel
the world
and worlds beyond
this one
I do not mean
simply
by airplane
flying
that would be
too easy
but living
after dying
flying
by believing

Astronaut

that woman
is some kind of astronaut
she will rocket you
straight to the moon
and have you dancing
in the craters
of her heart

blast off

TO THE MOON

I would have
chased the stars with you
if it meant
I could fly to the moon

I would have
danced on the moon with you
if it meant
touching both worlds
at once

DISTANT PLANETS

away he faded – future hope stranded
on faraway planets, suspended and banded
fate strung him up by a noose
hanging further away
shards of my universe
I truly hoped would stay
I thought would be mine
quickly pulled from my grasp
I believe we were cursed
now this lifetime will pass
a new one will look on in wonder
be dazed in a sense of awe
for them I dread the moment
frozen time will thaw

in the same gaze as mine
beneath him and up to him
I dreamt of colors entwined
in the tease of a fantasy that only lived
within a state of purple – I painted in my mind

making wishes, dreams on him
like I once did
on distant stars of blue
how do you tell them
you cannot contain a galaxy
how do you tell them
wishes on dying stars
do not come true

STARS

stars
fell into
your eyes and
suddenly you were a
galaxy
I called
my home – you
comfort of the embracing
universe
around me
colliding until I
became one with the
stars

TREASURES

if stars could fall into my arms
I would tuck them safely
away from harm
only peeking
to remind myself
I am one
of them

STARFIRE

she fights battles in her mind
separate from the physical
that nobody knows about
every single day
she conquers, she defeats, she wins
do not tell her
that she is anything but
a warrior
that she is anything less
than a fighter
that her soul is anything dimmer
than starfire
she is a goddess
she is
a survivor

Collapsing

my silent supernova killer
I drift into a state of numb
my mind – an even darker realm
cosmic shadows will soon come
the light inside me faintly flickers
a constant battle to reignite
I close my eyes while bracing myself
surviving another black night
scream into darkness if I have to
imploding and exploding by curse
stars collapse into themselves often
wake tomorrow, I will be a universe

rest tonight, reignite tomorrow
I am collapsing into my mind today
but tomorrow – I will ignite
if only, after a peaceful
well-rested night

OMNISCIENT

she sings silent songs to the silver moon
see Luna rising, a spotlight on she
a grand performance of a siren wishing
for more than her words will ever be

she sings for hope
forgotten dreams
to her surprise
the stars begin to gleam

shocking and sudden the skies erupt
into a spectacular choir of their own
symphonic cosmic beings sing
messages from her home

together she rises with them
on aurora of melodic resonance
as the curtain of midnight closes
moon fades into crescent

she is reborn into the light
a supernova omniscient

DIVINE

you are divine
straight to your bones
your body is a shelter
a powerful home
what lies inside
is all that you are
all that you are made of
a collection of stars

no one can dim your light
steal sparks or fade you
imagine the universe
growing, expanding
as you do
now open your eyes
gaze into a mirror
behold a divine being
the entire universe
that is you, dear

WE ARE LOST

soul mates exist, lost among stars
we are stars, lost among humanity

DREAM WITH ME

dream a dream with me
far from this reality
meet me there, my love

fly away with me
drift sweetly into slumber
find me there, my love

chase the stars with me
only us, our souls entwined
love me there, my love

THINK

if you held the world
in just the palm of your hand
would you destroy it
or guard it safely
knowing you held all of life
I would protect it

we all have this world in our hands

STAR PEOPLE

calling all wandering stars
who have different names
find me in the cosmos
we are of the same

I will grasp you, arms open
for I am wandering too
we will form our own galaxy
share the same moons

we are made of the universe
star stuff and star dust
you are never alone
in divine union we trust

TAKE ME HOME

fly me to the moon
I am wild among the stars
find me there, my love
I will fall like they do
a wish granted
into your arms

WONDERWALL

I embroidered myself
with a wall of wonders
weaved constellations
into the fibres of my soul
I used it as a shroud of warmth
wrapped tightly to protect me
worn often, time tore holes
a wonderwall repaired in patches
cloaked by my reality of dreams
with precision and satisfaction
I hid from the world in its seams

Whispers

if stars could speak
what would they say?
would they sing, laugh
scream at last
I believe
they are whispers
in the dark

JOINED

I fooled myself
into believing a soul mate
walked this earth among mortals
I am certain they are somewhere
trapped in the stars
just waiting to be reunited

SUPERNOVA

how can you doubt
that magic exists
between us

when we ourselves
are forged from the fires
of the same star

DEFENSE

in my defense
I can only claim
a mind of mad
hopeless romanticism
a heart full
of magic
and a soul
burning hotter
than all the suns
in the universe
for you

Cosmic Idiot

he seems to think I owe him
everything under the sun
he seems to think he is the sun
to him, I am but a miniscule speck
of space dust
revolving around him
cursed to his gravitational pull
I hate to extinguish his burning ego
but I think I'll have a go
I was made by the power of the cosmos
never will I be by him
he is colder than all of the moons
of Jupiter combined – lame and barren
I am capable of producing warmth
to heat hearts with love on a whim
I generate my own light from the very stars
flowing in my veins – gifted to me by creation
I do not owe him anything
the universe is not indebted to itself
I do not need permission
to ignite and shatter his confines
of an extraterrestrial prison
he is not entitled to my otherworldly intricacies
or my body, my presence – a prize to win
this speck of space dust is but a collapsing star
being manipulated for far too long
made small by his hands from afar
until, when I have had enough
I will erupt into the night
a supernova emerging by my own power
I will stand and fight

Torn Between

finding my sanctuary is as difficult
as claiming my sense of sanity
recalibrating my compass to no end
searching for grounding repeatedly

I do not know why I fight it
pull myself out of this state as if sin
this is simply a part of my being
faced with reality, my dreams always win

torn between keeping my mind
from swimming with the stars
diving into the depths of me
and drowning into the dark

why – can I not
please – can I not
have both
a malevolent conflict inside of me
driven by wild seas of hope

I was not born to tread shallow water
nor to soar in stagnant air
an ethereal soul is meant to thrive
by simply existing everywhere

Torn Between II

I cannot fully express how difficult and frustrating it is to stay afloat, grounded, and present when my mind constantly feels as if it is being torn between multiple planes of existence. Sometimes, I wish someone would pull me back to reality. Sometimes, I wish someone would take off with me. I'm holding on for dear life, either way.

pull me back to reality
soar with me into infinity
but please – do not
leave me hanging
in nothingness

BALANCE

this fragile heart of mine
is uniquely powerful in its creation
stitched together with starlight thread
forged within the infinite fire of the sun
cleansed by the churning seas of time

and I have felt it bleed
gilded miracles of molten love
erupting through the cracks

running on empty, I repair myself again
energizing my fragments with the stars
I wait for the soul who will pour into mine
balanced – by unity, we replenish our hearts

A LITTLE BIT OF EVERYTHING

my mother asked her mother
before she flew into paradise

"is there anything you need?"
heavy tears filled her eyes

"a little bit of everything"
she replied, and she sighed

her last breath was
that little bit
of everything
my mother cherished
in her life

*in loving memory of my Baba
who, as the strongest woman I have known,
still inspires me every day;
these were her last words to my mother*

*I think... we all need a little bit of everything
to survive*

STARGAZING

even as space dust and stars
fall from the sky on fire
they are gazed upon
as something wondrous
spectacular – beautiful
that is how I hope
to be remembered
maybe someone
will make a wish on me
when I fall out of life's orbit
blazing across the sky

DARLING, PLEASE

so darling, please scream
let the voids of oblivion shatter
the universe is listening to you
your powerful voice matters

so darling, please let go
of the painful binds on fire
you deserve love and freedom
fly away – soar higher

so darling, please breathe
evict the dust from your lungs
rest past ashes and flames
inhale the peace you have won

so darling, please live
this beautiful life is your own
I believe in your infinite magic
the stars are calling you home

Belief

I believe in the restoration of sunrise skies
I believe in the closure of sunsets and goodbyes
I believe in infinite beginnings and ends
I believe in the wisdom the universe sends
I believe that the universe is within us all
I believe in the fairy tales our own stories draw
I believe in happily ever afters
I believe in the connection of souls through disasters
I believe in falling wishing stars
I believe that god is a goddess of feminine art
I believe in the power of women
I believe that the elements heal us by diving in
I believe that life forms exist on distant planets
I believe that hope will never truly vanish
I believe that mothers are real superheroes
I believe that my daughter is a miracle
I believe that there is beauty in tragedy
I believe that the past builds us stronger rapidly
I believe that happiness is a choice
I believe that we are always finding our voice
I believe in the tranquility of loneliness
I believe in ethereal messages
I believe that forgiveness sets you free
I believe in love
I believe in magic
I believe in you
I believe in me

what do you believe in?

ENTITIES

exotic eccentricities
extract endless electricity
every entity entertains
enamoured epiphanies
even entwined elegance
each euphoric eminence
entering eyesight eternal
erupts ethereal evidence

PAUSE

time travels too fast
it feels like just yesterday
I met my daughter

a real miracle
blink – and suddenly she grows
wildhearted, like me

the dreams that I see
when I look into her eyes
reflections of mine

I know she will thrive
there is no doubt in my soul
she will weave wonders

there is one thing, though
that I wish I could control
if I could freeze life

I would hold her close
safe in my arms forever
and never let go

a mother's true love
transcends space and time
our hearts are combined

Loss

death has a way
of altering your perception
a heavy grief-filled reminder
to embrace every moment
every chance to say "I love you"
every laughing smile shared
every dance with your family
being thrown into the air
there will never be another
moment quite like it
one day there will be nothing more
when souls leave human frames
memories are all that we have left
to carry our loved one's remains
they have run out of tomorrow
while we are still left with today
how I wish I could pull them all back
it is inevitable nothing gold stays
sometimes you don't get answers
closure is an unknown concept
sometimes you don't get goodbyes
I never did, lost time my worst regret
I can only hope angels feel peace
resting with a life well-lived
free flying between both planes
reuniting with all lost kin

love you bunches, grandpa

BABA

my grandmother's home
was much like her heart
full of warmth, open arms
not an ounce of dark
she loved with all she was
despite endless struggles
a pure soul unchanged
by life's muddy puddles
she cooked for her family
bellies full of love
sometimes I still smell
the taste of heaven above
a true warrior woman
she fought battles ever strong
only peace she deserved
I remember her
in my mother's grieving song

the world isn't the same without you
neither are we
I miss you every day

OCTOBER 24

happy birthday, Dad
wherever you are
I hope you are carefree and smiling
if you could see me now
you would be so proud
I made it through, I'm surviving
I'm doing what I love every day
just like you told me I would
my daughter is happy and thriving
you believed in me, that I could
I can't help but wish
you were still here
there is so much I need to say
I wish I could have said goodbye
one more long talk, one more cry
I know you are still with me
in some form, some way
but I miss you especially
with tears in my eyes
and a wish for you
on your birthday

thank you for believing in me, Dad
I love you

MY LIGHT

my daughter, you come from
a long line of strong women
already I can see it in you
no matter where you go in life
my love for you remains true

I hope you chase stars
dance upon the full moon
little butterflies kiss your face
with the same happiness you give me too

you will always be my sunshine
even when skies are grey
rainbows will embrace you
to keep you safe
in my heart you will always stay

I love you to the moon and beyond

you are made of the universe
full of endless light
never stop shining
my twinkle star in the night

ECLIPSE

remember
the sun
how it feels
to share warmth with
her

remember
the moon
how it feels
bathing under light of
him

remember
their eclipse
how it feels
to embrace each other
us

DEAR WANDERERS

a soul's journey is a long-beaten path
through this lifetime into the next
it is also a tireless expedition
blooming with love and hope
a story of adventurous healing
unexpected twists and turns
hiking up infinite mountains
to take in the entirety of the universe
at the peak of your existence
it will take all of your strength
all of your courage, all of your magic
to bring you there
I believe in you
I know it is not easy chasing galaxies
your heart will soar with the stars
mind lost in the dark spaces in between
let me remind you gently
your soul has always been with you
inside you and guiding you
in the palms of your shaking hands
unsteady feet and quivering lips
keep opening every doorway ahead
do not be afraid of the unlit paths
you will find a way to illuminate them
with every step you take as you always do
through the maze of your life
through the doorways of your soul
until you find paradise
keep going
I'll meet you there

MOON WISHING

tonight
I am wishing
on the full moon
and every star
this wish
needs endless light
to reach
where you are

wherever, whenever, that may be

Vampirism

tell me
you taste stars
in my veins
and I will tell you
your bloodstream
carries a universe
just the same

let me drink from you

Bound By Thunder

to fall lovestruck is to be bound by thunder
electric paralysis coursing through twisted veins
sanguine enchantments promise longing of no other
spirited eyes arouse pearlescent pain

uncertainty restricts me and I am lost to oblivion
mischievous flattery burns bitter like the wind
these remnant dreams of infinite explosions
annihilate my breakable soul as I transcend

aftershocks that follow are devastating reminders
of the woven disillusion I was forced to believe
abhorring the very paradise that struck my blinders
still I beg to the skies – please don't leave

his malevolent force cut like lightning for reason
to deny love strengthened me, would surely be treason

Universe, Take The Wheel

once the soul starts to finally give into
and understand the natural course of life
the universe will always be in its favor

it is never the physical body failing
that will trigger a series of incredible events

it is complete surrender of your soul to the universe
saying, "let what is meant to be in this lifetime, be."

and it will hurt incredibly

existential crisis

not giving up, just giving in

RESILIENCE

I may crumble, but never disintegrate

I may stumble, but never collapse

I may retreat, but never disappear

I may surrender, but never attack

this life will not break me

nor will those who have tried

every downfall has a stronger rising

despite the odds, I'm still alive

FOREVER HOMES

darling, do not tell me
that I cannot live
without you
I am not foolish enough
to place my life
my happiness
my peace
my comfort
into the hands of another
I breathe my own breath
I circulate my own blood
I face my own fears
I keep myself warm
I was born without you
I can live without you
I will die without you
my will to survive is mine alone
that power you cannot claim
not my body, nor my bones
I learned a long time ago
to love myself alone
and most certainly
not to make crumbling humans
into forever homes

BELIEVE

a life of magic
is not hard to find
close your eyes
and open
your mind

ZEPHYR

in a land of make believe
there is a ship that lives in the sky
her name is Zephyr zeppelin
and through the air she flies

collecting souls of young and old
to lift their spirits high
she carries them away in dreams
and makes them feel alive

Zephyr has no order or captain
she drifts among the stars
on some nights, if you make a wish
she'll come and find you as you are

up among the sparkling clouds
where night and day cease to exist
the secret to her magic, though
she visits only who death has kissed

ABOVE ALL

we crash and we collide
creating constellations by genocide

we weep and we wither
wishing on star trails that shimmer

we hope and we hold
healing trauma young and old

we lighten and we learn
leaving legacies to eternally burn

we gleam and we glisten
giving hearts reason to listen

we love and we love
loving transcends all of the above

My Guiding Light

my evening and morning star
the gentle melody that echoes
from my fierce beating heart
my beloved beacon of hope
a divine reason to forever guard
your guiding light through the dark
my warmth and comforting arms
a soul sparking jealousy of the gods
I promise protection from all harm
against any otherworldly odds
my reason for living
breathing and thriving
you are worth the effort
it takes in surviving
my calm and my quiet
my wild and my wisdom
of all the magic in the universe
my daughter, I treasure you first
my sunlight and brightest days
my moonlight and starry nights
this is but only a twinkle
of the wonder and beauty
you have bestowed upon my life

Love, Mama
xoxo

Ghost

I don't know how many times
throughout my life
since I was young
I repeated and raised my voice
when asked what was wrong
why I was upset
what ate at me inside
it was never understood
only brushed aside
I stopped explaining myself
because it was ignored
nothing changed
nobody heard
a silence grew inside of me
now, all I have left
are these words
and I became
a ghost
even to those
I loved the most

still, to this day, to them, as I bleed
I'm not worth the effort
it takes to read

METAMORPHOSIS

I have never been one to place my heart into the hands of another to repair it after it has been broken, for fear of it being broken even more, or handled without care. Would they hold me protectively, or let me slip through their fingers? Would they take their time with a gentle touch, or crush me in their fists? I knew where the pieces belonged. I knew how to mend my wounds. I knew how to save myself. I've done it many times. I have the scars to prove it. But, sometimes, I wondered what would happen if I did – take every piece I have and surrender myself to someone else. Someone real. Someone fearless of my sharp edges. Someone capable, skilled, willing to help me heal with the love my heart needed and deserved. It would be a completely different heart, after all. And I think... it's time for a change.

even if it fails, I know now
that I can put myself back together
it is worth the risk

WAKE UP

I fight
every morning
to free myself from this
a state between reality
and dream

LIVING FOR LIFE

live
and live life
when you live for life
all lives become well-lived
and life is always
worth living

IGNITE

she will ignite by the firebreath of dragons
and rise on the wings of her dreams

INTERSTELLAR

intergalactic interconnectedness
spans lightyears away
across the universe
in spacial distances
flickering foundations
of extraterrestrial expansiveness
reminds us that we are not alone
in our cosmic and stellar existences
connections crafted are creating
subconscious omnipresence
tempting and toiling
time-space continuums
synchronic instances
serendipitous coincidences
soothe souls into surrender
by supernatural messages
we must learn
in our lust-wandering longing
to open our minds
and listen to their calling

STARCHILD I

I hope the stars
fall into your eyes
and the night sky
reflects the beauty
of all that you are

I hope the moon
only glows brighter
because of your light
and you dance upon it
to your heart's desires

I hope the sun
always guides you
and reminds you
of your power
but you will always be
the center of my universe
my beautiful daughter

STARCHILD II

I hope the planets align
and you skip across them
a path leading to other worlds
bringing endless hope
to all life forms often

I hope the floating stardust
turns into playful butterflies
and you chase and catch them
with pure joy in your eyes
while they lift you up higher
and into euphoria you fly

I hope the universe
that resides inside your soul
always reminds you
that you are never alone
we share the same stars
never lightyears apart
my daughter, you are the magic
of my cosmic heart

THIS OR THAT

I have a haunting, intangible fear
of immanent, impending death
of myself, of those unknown to me
of those I love and hold dearest

I live in a state of concealed panic
full of fleeting serendipities and
hasty decision, lest something bad
were to occur at any given moment

my soul is sentimental to everything
wondering if this, or if that
would be the last time
for this, or for that

it is the fear of suddenly losing
that purpose which keeps me alive
and when all is gone, what will be left
after striving so hard to survive

one thing is a certain constant, though
I will ward off any this, or any that
any danger which should arise
to keep my daughter protected
long after I have died

in motherhood, our fears
tend to grow stronger as our children grow older

Atomic

high-functioning atomic whirlwind
the next day, an imploding bomb
flip a mental switch and I turn off
dead in my tracks a distorted song

passive aggressive overtones
another manic obsessive episode
sinking into depression blind-sighted
pulled in by my own undertow

I used to be a well-trained expert
in forcing to forget, numbing myself
until everything catches up to me at once
afraid and struggling to ask for help

a lifetime of events made me this way
one after the other, it runs in my genealogy
I know I have fought to make it this far
some of my loved ones could not

I must tear open my wounds to heal properly
though I dread digging under my surface
I will do what it takes to be happy
there is hope for my soul, I have purpose

my life, my mind, my family
depend on me
I am not giving up today

I'LL BE DAMNED

drifting into solitude's fortress, I embrace my stars
specks of divinity floating in the aether – specks of me
enlightened by the presence of their light from afar
a mystery unanswered, content with where I may be

consciousness is revoked by my lust for damnation
the afterlife for heavenly sinners – sinners like me
in peaceful serenity reaching for empty temptation
every star in the universe, a soul to be set free

there is no daylight or night in the realm of a memory
secret havens for the lost ones – lost parts of me
I fall deeper into the madness of unspeakable treachery
witnessed and survived, darkness devoured and reaped

my chains are now starlight bound in mind and soul
free of him, yet eternally trapped in abyssal hold

BEYOND HELP

the damage done, I fear
may be irreversible
beyond therapeutic healing
wounds beyond the mind
are far more complex
than those of stripped flesh
temporary bandages, yes
small spurts of happiness
last for a moment and I am
again, unravelling
no reset switch can repair this
mental state of weighted abyss
my mind has been contorted
mangled, abused, manipulated
broken free of him – but memory
memory cannot be erased so easily
the after effects of a torturous hold
without an escape, I implode
into chaotic oblivion
and I fear that I am only a star
among a sea of souls
like me
who have drifted too far
waiting
to find the light within them
again

It's Complicated

I can't seem to decide
if I want to scream skyward
set myself, my world, on fire
until every star explodes and ignites
watching in devilish delight
or
if I want to scream into your ears
melody of a siren, waterfall tears
seductive symphonies of both
the stars – you
lost in me

if one might dare to dream
would I drag my sharpened claws
across a blank-canvas universe
creating streaks of wishful destiny
tearing a portal of opportunity
into the sheets of space and time
between us – to make you mine
or
scorch your flesh as I do best
leaving scarred remembrance
of me; fingertips carved into your chest
reaching, tearing, at your heart
drowning in carnal sweat
tempting our fate into a familiar
sinful, passionate bed

or would I simply stay silent
while I imagine
our bodies colliding in my head

BLAZE OF GLORY

I was
like an open-petalled flower
awakening with the dawn
like a moth drawn to a flame
in the dark and cold of night
like a defiant, wanderlust Icarus
flying head-on, wax wings wide, into the sun
like an immortal shooting star
burning beautiful, granting wishes
to the hopeful, the appreciative
of me

all of me seeking to be one with
to be warmed by, to hold onto
the light
fully aware and uncaring
that what I fought to survive for
live for, believe in, hope for
could slowly kill me mid-flight

still, I bloomed
still, I searched
still, I flew
still, I burned
and I will go down in flames
with a blaze of glory

remember my name
remember my story

SURVIVAL

1. walk away;
from the monsters
who drag you back –
from the bait poisoned
with sinister intentions
and darkened motives.

2. let go;
of those who weigh you down –
of those who intentionally enjoy
keeping you from reaching
your dreams.

3. break free;
from those who chain you
to them and refuse to let you fly –
escape their prisons, soar.

4. heal;
the damage and pain
those monsters inflicted on you
without a care, while you cared
infinitely too much.

5. live;
freely and unapologetically
far away from them
and what broke you –
live and breathe your dreams,
not their nightmares.

6. speak;
your story, your truth –
not what falsehoods they have said about you
to cover up their unforgiveable actions.

7. burn it all down;
throw a match into the past
and keep yourself warm
by the memory of only those dying flames.

8. fight;
to keep surviving every single day –
keep your mind and sword sharp,
keep your army close to your heart,
and slay any beast that ever tries
to overpower you.

9. survive;
because tomorrow is always worth seeing
and you are worthy of loving and being loved –
you are enough. reignite yourself.

10. remember;
you are not what happened to you
you are not their abuse
you are not your trauma
you are not them
you are alive for a reason
and that reason is to live a better life
after them, without them
for yourself.

OBSTACLES

don't let anyone throw you off of
or sabotage your unique route to healing
because they are unable to heal themselves
on their own twisted, mangled path
keep moving forward
and don't look back
anything behind you
is not worth losing your focus
slowing your pace, or going off track

with wicked smiles, they will boast and bleat
as you fall with weighted past's chains
wrapped tightly around your weary feet
to see you fail at their bloody hands
brings delight to evil eyes
demanding to be given the first prize
with false dignity and a foolish lead

there is no medallion or trophy to be stolen
it is your soul, it is you, who is inherently golden
overcome your own obstacles
without competition
for in surviving, there is never defeat
under any condition

BURN THE SKIES

shine your soul brighter
than the flames of hell
they tried to burn you in
don't be afraid
to set the night sky
on fire

let it rain down like witchcraft
wounded woman's scorned wings
crackling embers of our pyres
emerge – dance – scream – sing

burn the skies
burn the woven webs of lies
burn the beast, destroy it alive
burn every monster in disguise

rise from our ancestral ashes
raise your sanctuary an empire
an inferno accelerated
by survival
and desire

REVOLUTIONS

with a soul like Saturn
I will wrap the truth around me
like the stardust rings
that keep me protected
and I will speak it
in every revolution of my lifetime
around the sun

with a heart like Jupiter
I will love enormously
furiously, with my entire body
and I will learn to love
the storm that lives inside me
in every revolution of my lifetime
around the sun

with a mind like Earth
I will live a balanced existence
so that I may breathe creation
into the miracle of my life
never freezing, never burning
sustainably centered
in every revolution of my lifetime
around the sun

my spirit will be that of the universe
encompassing all that lives within it
I will manifest into my wildest wonders
and I will be beautiful infinite
in every revolution – of all of my lifetimes
with the power of every sun

LIGHTHOUSE

her eyes could set fire to the coldest abyss
arise flames of the darkest soul with her kiss
pull stars from the sky with a screaming wish
this was both her power, and her weakness

for eternal flames still burn bright
beyond the dead of a silent night
in dreams, her only source of light
was lit by the beacon of his

PRAYING FOR SUNLIGHT

the worst of winter is over
and still I am so
painfully cold
I'm shaking
I'm shivering
frozen into my bones
my hands feel like ice
a tundra under my skin
no, I am not sick
I just hate to admit
no amount of blankets
can compare to it
to the longing
for warmth
to be held
in loving arms

I used to love the cold, now, it's all I feel

CERTAINTIES

I can believe in magic
everything happens for a reason
and sometimes
wishes do come true

I cannot save myself
from everything
surviving my own mind
is the hardest to do

I do not know
what the future holds
but while I still hope
I hope I'm holding you

I know I shouldn't love him
it is mortally forbidden
but god damnit
I do

FEARLESS

I am not afraid
to fall hopelessly in love
with a deserving soul
to find happiness again
and that, despite it all
is bravery

I am not afraid
to face the mangled past
remember bridges burned
for harsh lessons learned
and that, despite it all
is wisdom

I am not afraid
to pull myself from darkness
because I know my heart
will always beat starlight
and that, despite it all
is strength

I am not afraid
to life my life powerfully
truthfully, ferociously, loud
never silenced into hiding
and that, despite it all
is survival

I am not afraid
to remove toxicity from my life
stand my ground, never settle
no matter how much
I may love someone
and that, despite it all
is courage

I am not afraid
to raise my daughter a fierce warrior
overcoming her battles tenfold
so that she may walk
her path of life fearlessly
with her head held high
and that, despite it all
is motherhood

I am not afraid

to be a woman

I am not afraid

to be me

SIMPLE THINGS

I am a lover of the simple things
I like nature, quiet, and birds that sing
curling up in a cozy blanket, listening to the rain
I am sentimental about emotions
not materials and expensive rings
too many lit candles and music soothes my soul
solitude is my sanctuary; I don't mind being alone
I like love notes, holding hands, and passionate sex
I prefer comfort at home and an early night's rest
sunsets and sunrises mesmerize my mind
a cup of coffee and a crossword is my good time
intelligent conversations stimulate all of my senses
I love to share smiles and laughter endless
poetry is my escape and I love reading books
falling in love with a soul is much stronger than looks
being a mother is the pride of my life
a large glass of wine can calm any strife
I stare hopefully, longingly, at every full moon
and with all simple things
they are gone too soon

TO BE SAVED

I refuse to believe

that the heart can't be healed
by the love of another
that the mind can't be mended
by the thoughts of another
that the soul can't be saved
by the embrace of another
that the body can't be bedded
by the desire of another
after it has been broken

and just when you start to believe
that you've exhausted all efforts
to survive on your own
unable to be saved – to be loved
you are meant to be alone

another will emerge
as if a wish from the stars
to prove you wrong, to give you hope
to remind you who you are

to you, they will say
that you can be saved
and you will be loved
by another one day

Miracles

surely, I can believe
that magic exists

I've seen it
I've felt it
I've touched it
I've held it

in the most mundane
and the most extraordinary
worldly and universal
miracles of my life

all of which exist
while loving you
all of which I see
in your eyes

in all of this, I find magic

Particles

in my dreams, we became one
and my vision flashed like starlight
raining from the heavens upon us
in an instant our souls collided
particles merging into a single entity
electric storms crackled under my skin
breath became frantic, frozen in time
we transformed – evolved – into a supernova
I, your guiding light – you, my hopeful dark
exploding together in orgasmic euphoria
trembling in your arms
taste of glistening skin
rising together, ascending within
every thrust a galaxy in first bloom
every gasp – moan – a sonic boom
floating along blissful oblivion sea
gaining speed, increasing in heat
I open my eyes
still feeling you
with me

FUCK THE STARS

run to me, my love

if the stars do tempt us, love
with a match made in perfection
let us then tempt the teasing stars
ignite sparks and burn the heavens

for the stars are fluent in cruel-fated love
ensuring nothing mortally golden lasts
the universe was surely foolish enough
to place you along my ravaged path

even if the stars do forbid this love
I will seek to unite my soul with yours
destiny can be altered, persuaded
to twist nature's plan off course

leap into the unknown with me, my love
even if the skies fade, collapse around us
have heart's faith in what we will it to be
our limits in each lifetime are boundless

run to me, my love

let us create new worlds
in the arms of our desire
if we go down in flames, my love
let it be by soul's fire

Sounds That Stir My Soul

absolute silence / 5 a.m. birdsong / coffee brewing / snowfall at night / wind in the summer / crows cawing / cats purring / babies sleeping / my daughter's first cry / a man's gentle voice / careless laughter / waterfalls roaring / symphonies / motorcycles after winter / waves on the beach / candle wicks crackling / passionate moans / cigarettes lighting / duct tape unravelling / rain pelting a window / thunderstorms / ice falling from trees / rush hour traffic horns / zippers / emergency sirens / snow melting / wine pouring / beer opening / barbeque sizzles / ribbon curling / airplane propellers / engines starting / crunchy Autumn leaves / pleasurable sighs / doors locking / footsteps leaving / muffled voices / anything but my thoughts / "I love you" / "goodbye" / the sound of silence.

TO BE RESPECTED

to be wanted, not for my physical beauty
but for my soul, what I love and believe in
I am a woman, a mother, a daughter, a sister
know me, all that lives beneath my skin

to be touched, not by prying greedy hands
not by dirty fingers, or crude, vain remarks
but only with consensual, genuine caresses
enough to fill the world with respectful hearts

to be desired, not for my youthful breasts
or for my vagina, or exposed supple skin
but for my profound confidence as a woman
together, let our power inspire a revolution

to be seen, as never a violent conquest
not a prize to be claimed on a pedestal or won
not a body to be bedded or forcefully wedded
not a womb to be owned or raped for fun

I wish for us women to be treated
with equality, the feminine ferocity we exude
do not touch us without our permission
whether we are fully clothed, or fully nude

a world where we are no longer ravaged
taken by force against our will is not too late
we deserve to wake up each morning and live
peacefully, believing we are safe

It Is Possible

to take the risk in opening, unlocking
the cage around your battered heart
(or rather, what's left of it)
is exposing it blindly to someone
who has the power given by you
to repair or shatter
the pieces remaining
to choose to run away
or stay

for you to say – this is me, I am not perfect
but I will love you with every shard
I have left in me

and the light shines through their eyes
and they take your damage as their own
and they admire all that you endured
and they hold you in their arms
and they are not afraid of you
and they want to stay
and they love you
and they care
and you are
safe

this
is magic

STILL BURNING

oh, darling
if you believe lighting a match
will burn me upon your stake
you best prepare yourself
to face the fire I become
when a goddess rises
in my place

BLAZING

I am blazing, stark-raving mad
heavenly, heartbreakingly bad
extreme, explosively sad
intensely iron clad

I am blazing, burning crazy
insane, insensitively lazy
overwhelming, obsessively hazy
daring, disastrous daisy

I am blazing, magic one
frantic, flirtatious, fatal fun
hopeless, harmless, guarded gun
sexual spitfire, siren sun

I am blazing, fiery hot
weak woman, I am not
incessant imperfections rot
starlit soul, suffering in thought

SAVE ME

hold me, salvation
until dark evolves into light
stay with me

I HAVE LEARNED

oh, brave heart
take pride in protecting yourself
for you are still beating fiercely
with wisdom earned in every lesson
withstanding wild tempest storms
intruders of ill intent are warned
fury of a burning woman scorned
stars surround you and keep you warm
growing forth through murky denial
conqueror of life's love trials
fail not, my dear soul
you are triumphant
in survival

STILL, I DREAM

purple was real once
only existent to me
my soul entwined
to another
or so, I believed
a vision I carry
hopelessly
pulled from my realm
of impossible dream

ETERNAL

stars, ignite my fires
let my wishes be granted
heed my deep desires

tame not my wild heart
for whilst I live and I breathe
hope will live in me

hide not in darkness
my soul smoulders with pure love
awaiting a spark

stars, entrust me fire
send me a twin inferno
blazing, eternal

I'M READY

tonight
I release the past
tonight
I am hopeful
tonight
I rest peacefully
tonight
I welcome love
tonight
I am happy
tonight
I am thankful
tonight
I am ready
for tomorrow
the sun rises with me
tomorrow
I let go

the night I finally said goodbye
to the last man who claimed my body
as his
and in the morning, I was saved by another

BANG

he said, baby
you're holding onto this love
so fucking tight
that you're killing it

but, my darling, need I remind you
that the very universe we reside in
was birthed under the pressure
of a single condensed particle
that exploded infinitely outward
throughout the darkest cosmos
into billions of burning stars
glittering galaxies
never-ending nebulas
limitless life forms
and it is still
expanding
to this day

my love
this is not our death
this is our creation

love doesn't die, it evolves

Heaven Sent

after years of crawling through hell
fighting every day just to survive another
giving up hope on ever being held again
rebuilding, repairing, what was broken
he came into my life unexpectedly
as if the universe knew what I needed
and in the same flash of light
I saw in his eyes
everything changed instantly
I felt a spark inside of me
that – finally
did not hurt
instead, it gave me hope
he saw my soul, and I his
in his arms my chaos settled
the past healed, walls crumbled
with only a kiss
he has seen my darkness and stayed
we are equally matched in all of this
everything we endured led us to salvation
two souls deserving of another's bliss
thank you, my sunlight, for finding me
my heaven-sent stormchaser
what a beautiful love this is

PLUTO

fly too close to the sun
you are bound to get burned

but I am a woman of fire
deserving of a love much hotter
than the faulty flares emitted
only when it is time for you
to burn with me in turn

my darling, I see now you are Pluto
too far, too cold, too distant
what potential I saw in you
to ever keep me warm
was simply an illusion

the fire I saw in your eyes
was a reflection of my might
for in loving you too fiercely
I was blinded
by my own light

THE STARS ARE DEAD

it's incredible how quickly
stars can die and explode
not because of outside force
but because they are simply
unable to contain the fire
inside them

and I was in the path of their destruction
with arms wide open

GOODNIGHT, SUNLIGHT

wishing on every star
would not bring us together
so, I will sleep atop the moon tonight
where you will find me forever

I await our eclipse, my sunlight

CHANGE THE STARS

if I could change the stars
I would pull you into my arms
never shall we be but a sparkle away
space would not dare tear us apart

if I could change the stars
I would dance into galaxies new
where I create purple with my soul
from heart's red, and mind's blue

if I could change the stars
I would not alter the past
a universe is seen in my dreams
where all forms of love will last

if I could change the stars
I would bring all who have lost closer together
so that all worlds will unite in endless sunlight
living peacefully, happily – forever

You Found Me Here

of all the stars in the sky
it was eternal destiny
granting us wings to fly
two wandering souls
colliding together
floating in space
as light as a feather
you have seen my darkness
you have felt my stars
hand in hand, we create
a universe that is ours
we wish upon burning hope
embrace by the sun's fire
hold me, my love
let us rise higher

THE SKIES ABOVE

and if you believe that you are falling
from the stars you were born of
flickering – descending to the earth
feeling like a lost comet crashing
grounded – imprisoned to the dirt
always yearning of returning home
you are still a blazing star's rebirth

allow yourself to rise and catch fire
free the binds of gravitational desire
scorch the shackles on your heart
ascend – reclaim your dormant spark

those that tried to confine
strip you of your peace of mind
will search their darkest nights
only to painfully find

that they could never claim you
or fathom to contain
the powerful supernova
that burns in your veins
the entirety of the universe
that is living inside of you
as the stars in your eyes
ignite the sky again

the seas below

if you feel like
you are drowning
dive further and deeper
into the depths
of yourself

OCEANS

if you asked me
what I have survived
a torrent of memories
would erupt behind my eyes
as I replay it all
a flash flood of emotions
carries me away
in unrelenting oceans
to put it very simply
I am a survivor of life
as are we all
fighting to survive
one
more
day

We are all survivors surviving the ocean of life every single day. Refusing to drown in its unexpected storms, and drifting calmly along its gentle waves

Keep swimming, we will find the shore

TIDAL

my love for you
will ebb and flow
like the tides
drawn by the moon
I hope you swim
strongly enough
before I pull you
under
too soon

I will drown you in me

I'm a bit reckless
slightly calm, a pretty mess
love me in my waves
swiftly kiss me
then
undress

OVERBOARD

I learned to swim
at a young age
through the tidal waves
of my life
I am not afraid
to cross oceans
to save myself
even if I am
tangled in seaweed
ripping at fisherman's nets
coughing up saltwater
I will drag myself
dripping
to shore

Ripple Effect

it begins

with a quake driven to my core

suddenly

small ripples form into waves

blink

and I am a tsunami

run

vengeful karma gives chase

Under Water

there are days when I feel
a little under the water
rather than under the weather
even on the most beautiful days
warm air and skin kissed by sunlight
that should make me feel brighter
but I don't
I could climb the tallest mountain of my life
and still feel as if I was drowning
below sea level atop an inverted peak
not knowing if I should panic
or be proud of myself
or both
I should feel invincible
but I don't
when it rains for days
I should be happy, relieved even
rain is weather under water after all
does it not cancel out the two?
I should be dancing in it
laughing and crying at the same time
but I don't
when it rains, nobody can tell the difference
between someone dancing
under the weather
or drowning
under the water

BACKWARDS CURRENT

if you must start over again
from where it all began
go back to your childhood home
take your wisdom and strength
and all you have gained with you
you are not walking alone
you've felt these familiar waters
you know its dangers well
this time it will not drown you
or wash you out
you will swim strongly on your own
and be carried off
into paradise

DIVE IN

drown me in your thoughts
a conversation with depth
let me swim with you

I'm a strong swimmer

LAKE LOVE

I could drown
in this moment
quench my thirst
with you
while dancing
in the depths I share
with you
and I, my love
if I drown
with you
I would still smile
without a care

DROUGHT

people change
like the tides
and your ocean
became a desert

once deep
thirst quenching
now dry
and relenting

you were my oasis

Hope And Help

what am I supposed to do
when my mind starts to wage war
against every cell of my body
my head feels trapped in a vice grip
yet exploding into infinity as I slip

I have people I love depending on me
I cannot let myself sink now
reverting back to painful insanity

after fighting strong for so long
surviving what might have killed me
through everything that went wrong
I fought hell and high water headstrong
instead of numbing it again
I braced myself – I held on

I do not want my happiness
to depend on medications
reality is real and I have faced it
there are no mental health vacations

giving up is never an option

maybe now, everything is catching up to me
maybe now, the pain needs to be set free
maybe now, I need a break from saving myself
maybe now, it's time to ask for help

Fɪsʜ

he thought I was his prized catch
caught me so quickly, so easily
wanted a challenge, to try again
for the thrill of his ego
liked watching me swim

tossed me back to the water
his hook nestled in my flesh
in case I tried to escape from him
a fish under net arrest

he reeled me back in
threw me back out
over and over

every time the wound tore deeper
until I finally freed myself
ripping him from my flesh and fate
as I swam away
from his fisherman's cage

THIRSTY

how frantic he becomes
when he feels me
slipping away
no longer in clenched fingers
I have shattered his cage
pulling me back
by the same hands
I escaped
grasping at tiny straws
finding another way
to sip
me in
again
but darling
I quite enjoy
drinking in my freedom
by swallowing
the waves

don't cage a mermaid

Slipping

I was never meant to be held
by the hands of greedy men
with fingers for cages
a survival technique
slipping myself gently
through their weak grasp
when they held me tighter
oh, the fury – when I escape
but I am of water, and I must
flow freely, beautifully
on my own

CATACLYSM

do not tone down your magic
for those who cannot contain
the enormity of your power
their hands can only carry
a miniscule spark
and my darling
you are the entire supernova
the cataclysm that follows after
and the wave of creation
that vibrates
across the sea of time

Shipwrecked

I could sail across
every sea and ocean
with confidence
and yet
find myself
shipwrecked
upon his shore
I came too close
to his jagged edges
only to find
a deserted island
nothing more

not even buried treasure

INSTINCT

I want to close my eyes
empty the air from my lungs
fall backwards – sink
into the dark below me
into the shadows that lurk inside me
into the depths that pull me under
just to see how long it takes
for me to remind myself
I could breathe
underwater
after all

*if you can't drown in the darkness of yourself
nobody else can drown you in theirs*

WOMAN, YOU ARE THE OCEAN

you deserve the same effort
the moon has given the sea
a strong current of desire
not a love in flaccid ripples
you deserve to be kissed
like the moonlight
kisses the elements
after your storm
has settled at night
a mirrored reflection
of tranquil luminescence
you deserve the depths of devotion
woman, you are the entire ocean
do not settle for a small wave on the surface
the man who loves you
will dive in, and swim with purpose
without fear or hesitation
as one with you
knowing underwater breathing
is a magic two can do

for the women who are tired
of those tiny little surface tickles
and being loved in waves
may they stop throwing stones into us
while making foolish wishes
always standing on the edge
afraid of what lies deeper

CASUALTIES

I told you
I would drown you
I know no other way
but to love
only deeply

I told you
I held storms in me
I never meant for you
to become a casualty
of my hurricanes

I told you
I warned you
I cannot calm
my tidal heart

I am a catastrophe
you should not
have crashed
into
my waves

to those I have hurt while loving
and feeling too strongly
and not enough at the same time
I'm sorry

Aquaman

my siren soul belongs to the sea
nautical heart eternally
singing wavelengths with the tide
calling, beckoning – for my wild love
as deep as the ocean within me
a companion to swim strongly with
one I can dive deeper into
forever

water keeps me alive and revived
a magic my Piscean veins carry
to return to my destined home
if ever lost – brought to sweet serenity

we breathe by freedom flowing
a dance together into the undertow
through the reflections above our descent
Luna blesses us with moonlit halos

I suffocate on the surface
I live to thrive in the depths again
and I am drowning in longing
reaching underwater
to be united
with my aquaman

BETWEEN WORLDS

waiting here
for him still
I will drown
exhausting
all efforts
suspended
between worlds
I can't live
in this state
break myself
from his curse
I can – will
to the wind
I will soar
higher now
without him
I am free
I am alive
somewhere in
rock bottom
letting go
breaking down
healing wounds
surviving
I found strength
I found hope
I found me

STORMS

the storms inside me
do not wish to be settled
instead – made stronger

bring your hurricanes
merge chaos into my heart
clear debris of past

let our disasters
birth wavelengths of creation
new life will flourish

the storms inside me
seek to unite with your own
together – stronger

SEA SALT

I can still taste
the salty air of the sea
sweet on my tongue
weightless inside me

I can remember
swift currents along my shore
the sound of waves crashing
into mine – into yours

I can still feel
the darkened force that came
polluting my sanctuary
adrift, I curse his name

I can remember
breaking barriers
through troubled water
swimming free from him
at last

tangled in seaweed
coughing up memories
alive – still breathing
I survived
the past

SEARCHING FOR ATLANTIS

when my parents separated
my heart felt like it sank
when I saw my father walk away
my hope felt like it vanished

love became elusive as mythology
buried into the depths of the abyss
I thought would never be found again
soon, I was my own forgotten Atlantis

I have been searching for my dreams
wandering ever since
jaded by arid human deserts
I believed to be genuine oceans
only to remind me that love
as they were – was a vast illusion

my life is a faded treasure map
searching for fragments of my heart
and I have been spinning in circles
for it only leads me back into the dark

I tore up that map a long time ago
creating my own path
that led me to a sea of stars
where I found my heart's home
my Atlantis at last

THE UNWORTHY

she was the ocean
but he
was afraid
of drowning

he demanded
to be loved deeply
but could only breathe
in the shallows
of the surface

he blamed her
when she gave him love
by the torrents of her depth
though she knew
he would not survive
for foolish men
bait their own death

she is the ocean
guarding eternity inside of her
a world worth discovering
by one truly capable
of diving in
first

CLAWS

I have chewed my claws back
to the quicks of my nailbeds
I have been sheathed and tamed
for far too long

I kept myself filed down and blunt
inflicting stinging pain onto my body
for fear of making others bleed
even those who have loved me wrong

I morphed when I finally strengthened
sharpened my teeth, armoured my heart
formed my backbone into a fortress
these daggers of mine grew as well

I was dragged through the dirt and buried
with raw hands I furiously dug myself out
I am not afraid now to use my claws
to tear those demons straight back to hell

Neptune

my soul is a treacherous whirlpool
I will lure and pull you into my seas
by the forces of Neptune's nature
curiosity will kill a fool in slow agony

gaze upon your unknown fate
feel temptation and feast on your fear
falling faster now, swim deeper darling
pray for survival – the end is near

what lies beneath is a trove of treasures
only the worthy can truly seek and find
if you can dive into my heart
with yours still beating
a challenge awaits you
in the storms of my mind

MASKED SIREN

I saw glimpses
through the mask he wore
dark eyes and a devilish smile
like a fool it left me craving more
I knew what was beneath his guile

a trickster of deceit he taunted me
flattery was his siren's work of magic
his cunning desire to lure me in
revealed a fate beautifully tragic

he pulled me
into the depths
with him
rescue was all too late

and I

oh, I did not
even try
to escape

FOUND AT SEA

it was during the darkest nights of my life
when I felt the world closing in around on me
I remember screaming
silently into the aether – please, help me survive
hoping for an answer and a reason
for me to keep holding on
to keep me alive

my eyes were closed so tightly
that I could see sparks of lightning
amidst the abyss I felt I was entering
fading by the embers in my lungs igniting

deep inside of me I knew that this
was the divine evolution that I asked for

soon the stars blazing in my mind
erupted and became a sea of tears
streaming down my pale face
there was nothing more I could possibly fear

drifting into instances of a drowning reality
I realised in the depths of my subconscious
that my stars are the ocean – I am of both worlds
I can survive anything
even the trenches of him

I smiled to myself triumphantly
and invited the universe
for a swim

POTENTIAL

darling, you are an oasis
capable of becoming
a geyser aimed skyward
a body of life-giving water
a deep expanding empire
do not allow yourself
to become a fountain
for the greedily thirsty
drained of all that makes you
the wonder that you are
preserve your power
expand your horizons
and in the twilight
your soul will reflect
the stars

Clockwork

we all reach our breaking points
when the mind wages war on our bodies
life becomes a vortex of draining energy
we only want to rest for an eternity
but the torment inside keeps us awake
wondering how much more of this
we can possibly take

I have accepted this epiphany
as a pendulum striking
upon the hour of change
this inevitable cycle that repeats itself daily
I recognize it personally by name
every second is a tick of anxiety
every minute a lull of depression
though the hours that stand out
on the bold faces of our lives
are important memories and lessons

now once again, the creeping hands
strike midnight's darkest hour
the clockwork will begin again
life may consume and devour
but our clocks never stop
fighting to move forward
and neither shall you
our time is precious, keep it ticking
until only chimes of peace ring true

UNFORTUNATE SOULS

I have always been drawn
to the tortured souls
the damaged, the broken
wandering souls
a part of me wants to dive in
and explore all that lives
under their life-ravaged skin
wishing that I could paint stars
to illuminate the darkness
in their hearts
yet I often find myself drowning
struggling to come up for air
if only they knew I was trying
to save them – that I care
I have had my light siphoned from me
and I hope that it was not in vain
if it helped at least in the slightest
to ease their burdened pain
healing is a torturous battle
I know this to be true
maybe it's simply because
I am one of them too

WALKING ON WATER

dreams of mine are enlightened bliss
walking on water in the twilight mist
hand in my hand, I reminisce
moonlit hope in his eternal kiss

dreams of mine do not last forever
walking on water a deadly endeavor
hand in my hand, our grasp severs
moonlit hope in his kiss – never

SHIFTER

I do not need saving
rescue or redemption
I have saved myself
many times
watching my soul
unravel
into a dark mass
melting into the shadows
every time without fail
I have congealed
altered state
evolving my form
into something powerful
different than before
a force of the opposite
call me a shape shifter
if you must
I am no stranger
to transformation
watch
me
change

ELECTRIC

I could feel
his presence approaching
anticipating the rising storm
when our skies grew wilder
tide rose higher, waves sharper
thunder roaring, wind howling
what once was a ripple in my heart
became a fast-moving behemoth
licking and lapping at my soul
oh, but my body was beckoning!
standing at the edge
of the highest rocky cliff
waiting for the lightning
to strike us both
until I jumped in
to meet him

shock therapy

OASIS

her body shifts
like the sands of time
inside an hourglass
of euphoria
a dance of the divine
she is an oasis
of all elements
a goddess
personified

ANXIETY

a panic in the morning
while opening your eyes
no, you are not drowning
only terror in disguise

something is going to happen
something is terribly wrong
I do not know what, though
mind and body fighting strong

just get yourself out of bed
snap out of it, you will be fine
every morning before life starts
anxiety attacks me, right on time

5 a.m.

THERE ARE DAYS

there are days
when I feel like submerging
my face into a bottomless well
full of nothing but my internal hell
and screaming until my lungs
render their twisted veins undone
expelling every ounce of oxygen
filling up with poison burning into them
closing my eyes
into a sea of black
and never climbing back
out

and there are days
when I am trapped in between
one foot in reality
one foot in dream

and there are days
when I emerge from the surface
free from the depths of misery's purpose
inhaling the hopeful, beautiful scent of life
the sun on my skin sparks me alive
my reason for living is cause to survive
I fight – I swim – I fight
I can see the light
I can feel the light
I open my eyes
and I am still
breathing

DUST TO DUST

the night we met, who knew the wolves in us would play
in the silver and cold, frosted crystal winter
I had fallen by your gravity like a landslide in slow decay
into your arms, you removed every jagged splinter

breathe me a love song, don't speak – let go
stay here with me now while we are sleeping to dream
our eyelids shut, yesterday's distance comes to a close
hearts trapped in jars of a stubborn love unseen

dust to dust, love within lust
shallow and unsteady, we part our ways
until you remember the overdose of loss in my trust
and why now, after everything, I'm not okay

we loved until night
our morning sun was brighter
ceased by our last fight

COURSE OF MY NATURE

rather than running
like the wind
I preferred to swim
like the waves
and perhaps, that is why
I have always crashed
violently into jagged rocks
carving out hollow caves
instead of gracefully floating
through innocent trees
kissing and tickling
their fluttering leaves

Sail

you will never find me
capsizing, begging on my knees
sinking my ship lower for a pirate
bending and breaking to please

my soul is a strengthened vessel
elegant morale within gilded sails
I trust the stars to guide me safely
and my heart's own treasured trails

you will never find me
held down by my anchor's weight
for I am sailing beyond mortal horizons
fulfilling a dream of seafaring fate

my soul is a strengthened vessel
free to roam to the ends of the earth
you will never find me
the ocean has found me first

EMERALDS

a greedy captor coveted the gaze of her eyes
believed to be once the ocean's most sacred jewels
prismatic and iridescent secrets in disguise
trapped in the unworthy, pestilent hands of a fool

in them, he knew of the treasures deeply hidden
one might find if they should fall upon her stare
a blindfold tautly sealed, bound in dark ribbon
kept his prized possession from others unaware

enter, behold, bravest and deserving of she
approach swift surely, anticipate her wonder
exile mortal binds and set rare beauty free
sight of gemstones indeed – a marvel to plunder

to the light, her soul rose upon freeing truth-bearing eyes
emerald enchantment felled the envious unto fate's demise

OBSIDIAN SHORES

I will love you
like the fresh lava flow erupting
from a long enduring volcano
once peacefully well rested
stirred from my slumber
by abrasive worldly friction
now slowly oozing, creeping
surrendering forward
towards you
an approach full
of infernal agony

I will love you
like the fresh lava flow seeping
longing to meet the cool black sea
when we touch, a ceasefire
settling your waves upon me
not a sound heard elsewhere
a private crackle between us
obsidian formed by serenity
a safe shore created
in elemental peace
only then, on this earth
will time freeze
my infernal agony
be released

a new shore
a new foundation
a new beginning

FREEDOM FISH

I
am not
a fish hooked
reeled in by poisonous
bait

I
swim far
away from him
free of polluted, toxic
cage

I
am not
a foolish fish
for in escaping, I
survived

I
swim strongly
away from him
to keep my soul
alive

I Hate You; I Love You

I hate you; I love you
please don't leave
I hate you; I love you
stay away from me

I hate you; I love you
in darkness that I breathe
I hate you; I love you
in light that helps me see

I hate you; I love you
to those I hurt, who have hurt me
I hate you; I love you
for attempting to break me

I hate you; I love you
I'm truly sorry

I hate me; I love me
for surviving haunting memories

I hate me; I love me
for having to set myself free

I hate me; I love me
for not giving up so easily

I hate me; I love me
every day that I breathe

F* You

I want to forget you

forget who you really are
forget everything you truly did
forget your permanent scars
forget all of your dirty secrets
forget all of your twisted sins
forget every wicked lie you told
forget your abyssal prison

I want to forget you

erase you entirely from my memory
because you will never be sorry
for the unforgiveable
hell
you have always given me

I will forget you

and I will finally live in peace

FLASH FLOODS

oh thunder, calm your rain
you cannot compete
with the storms in my brain
your roaring is a mere whisper
compared to the emotionally insane
my own flash floods have hit me
long before your lightning came
and I am drowning tonight fiercely
in my heart's torrential pain

the only force of nature I fight is myself

STILL HERE

I am overly obsessive, passive aggressive
extremely possessive, manic depressive
self-destructive, loving and lustrous
my soul has been torn
in every direction
and I am sorry
for wrapping you
around my messes
my sunlight, you save me
crumble my defenses
you kiss me and I am
closer to heaven
my storms have pulled you
under treacherous conditions
when I lose control
over all of my senses
still, you are here
I hear your voice in the dark
I'm here… still here… I'm still here
until it passes
until you hold me again
you are still here
with your soul
by my side

my sunlight, my stormchaser
my crazy

BLACK & BLUE

call me crazy
heartless
destructive
insane
label me
because I escaped
with your own
afflictions to blame

but when the next victim
asks you in reply
smart enough
to retain sympathy
seeing past your lies
she says to you
"what did you do to her then,
devil in disguise?"

I hope you answer
with the truth for once
I drove her
to her grave
and I enjoyed
every manipulative
degrading
punch

WHAT ABOUT YOU

who does he think he is?
believing that he can paint me
into a manipulated picture
by his venom-dipped, devil's paintbrush
a twisted caricature

who does he think he is?
entitled, so much, that he can tell
a one-sided story about me
hiding his own darkness
under a carefully placed veil

who does he think he is?
creating a version of me, my bones
that will never be called my own
failing to weave words that are true
sentenced by karma to a lonely life – alone

who does he think he is?
speaking for me instead of himself
calling me insane whilst over-blamed
until I believe it, thinking I am the one
who needs to seek mental help?

who does he think he is?
seeking to destroy me
because his abuse I escaped
who does he think he is?
I am no longer his prisoner
or his prey

DO IT, BECAUSE THEY SAID YOU COULDN'T

There are some things that hurt as much as (sometimes more than) the trauma itself. The after effects, the healing, the triggers, the memories. The list goes on.

One of these things is being pressured by those I love and have loved to stay silent about what happened throughout my life and not to tell my side of the story, the truth, that so many have tried to burn along with me.

I knew that speaking about it and letting my voice be heard would come with both positive and negative feedback like it has, and I took up my pen and raised my voice despite it all. Despite my abuser seeking revenge for speaking the truth that he had tried so hard to twist and conceal. As I wrote previously, "slavery, meet my bravery, as I set myself free."

I have been told a number of things including, "You shouldn't say anything about it/them/what happened," "Just let it go, it's done, move on," "Aren't you afraid he might retaliate, come after you again, hurt you more, exploit you, twist your story, etc.?" "Speaking about it will only give him more power over you," "Nobody will believe you," "It couldn't have been that bad." And the worst, "You deserve everything that happened to you in your life."

My answer: There is no more that they can do to me that hasn't already been said and done. I was dragged through hell and back. I know the truth, and what I have lived, felt, and experienced. My loved ones protect and support me, and they have witnessed the turmoil and after effects of those experiences first hand. I escaped to protect myself and my daughter. I deserve and have the right to defend myself, my integrity, and my dignity. I am no longer a victim – but a survivor. I will not live in fear any longer of my trauma or my past. I have a voice and I will speak it. I have a story to tell and I will tell it. I have a truth to be heard and I will let it be known. I have to do this for myself, for other women, and those I love and care about. This is how I take my power back. This is how I hope. This is how I heal. This is how I cope.

And I will not be silenced.

This is why we speak, because if we don't do it for ourselves, then nobody else will. Even if nobody believes it, or believes in you, you deserve to use your voice and fight for yourself, your survival, your peace, your happiness, your love, your family, your life, and your well-being.

This is me. This is my life. This is my story.

I will continue to tell it because they said I shouldn't, wouldn't, couldn't.

WE CAN, AND WE WILL

those who persistently try
to keep you in a toxic relationship
like a forced prison
by saying
'if you love me, you will never leave'
clearly have long-standing, lifelong
abandonment issues
and manipulation up their sleeves

if you think continued mistreatment
of those that do try to love you
will make them stay in misery
for the sake of a twisted love
you are sorely mistaken
they can and will leave
and you best let them

it doesn't matter how much
you truly love someone
if they give you every reason
to walk away
you are allowed to leave
without guilt projected
revenge taken
by their entitlement
and insecurities

FOR GOOD REASON

everything I ever did or have ever done
has been for my heart's survival
and protection
because a peaceful life
is not a prize or victory
it is a human right
that should not have to be fought for
and won day and night

I do not battle monsters
for fame, or for glory
this is my life
my daughter's life
every woman's life
I am fighting for
this is my truth
this is my story

TREASURE HUNT

spread me open, part my seas
sail my long, laguna length legs
with feverish tongue
starved, heavy lungs
let your waves roar into me
lick and lap against
soft and supple shores
swift breeze – more
trembling trees – more
body like a waterfall
reflecting beads
of diamond prisms
under sultry siren sun
tantalizing one
I beckon – come
I tempt – deeper
there is treasure
beneath the surface
serendipity seeker
start
exploring
me

x marks the spot

GIVE KARMA A KISS

emotionally abusive exorcist
gaslighting, gross illusionist
traumatic, psychological terrorist
coercion spell contortionist
manipulative maneuver – twist
into deranged, elusive extortionist
closeted monster, masked mortal cyst
narcissistic and manic neuroticist
possessive, secret sinister sadist
in liar's light, a holy virgin evangelist
truth be told – soul's sanity rapist
turning the faithful into victimized escapist
demon of dark, devouring, toxic mist
desperate attention-seeking, sickened socialist
life's loneliest sentence will be your only gift
stay far away from me
give karma a kiss

THE BEST

and if I was truly
the worst thing
to ever happen
to you
I hope you remember
I tried to be the best
for you

FIGHTING

I have no fight left
in me
to fight you

I'm killing the hate
so I can hold on
to the good

so my soul can heal

so I can be free

the only fight left
in me

is for me

ANCHORS AWAY

throw me overboard if loving him
means stumbling on a decaying plank
not knowing if it will break before me
for the rest of my treasured life

toss me to the shark's razor cages
and let them tear at my flesh
have their way with me
as they do best
a change of sensational scenery
from my soul he ingests

because loving him
is no different

than a predator tasting a drop of my blood
frantically craving more in a feeding frenzy
he is a ravenous, vengeful piranha
leaving nothing left of me
not even scraps of who I used to be
sweet sanity I can't take back
reeling me in, baiting me after I escape

so, sadistic sailor, anchors away
lure me into the depths
of my paradise, my watered-down grave
abandon all hope, your sinking ship
unforgiving storms have churned aboard it
you will be consumed, and I will be saved
by the ocean's karmic waves

THE CHASE

our love was a delicious sin
burning up in flames
too fast, too passionate
becoming enemies in a haze
two souls set on fire
by a flicker of twisted fate
until ignorance became
a poisonous, bitter taste
dying embers to the past
last of heart's forsaken chase

SURRENDER

the one who can hold
the fish
contain a woman
of the water
a woman who flows freely
with the power and depth
of the ocean
can only be a soul
she swims willingly toward

Parasite

those memories
the goddamn flashbacks
I can still feel him
under
inside
on top of
my skin
tearing at me
taking me
in waves
I am
crawling
s c r e a m i n g
get
out
of
me

please

IT ISN'T REAL

sometimes my dreams
are too good to be true
sometimes my dreams
drag me back to you

sometimes my dreams
play tricks on my mind
sometimes my dreams
are cruel and unkind

sometimes my dreams
fade into nightmares too fast
sometimes my dreams
are not destined to last

sometimes my dreams
are tickled in fantasy
sometimes my dreams
are better than reality

and sometimes I wonder
if you were really there
with me too
a state of peace
between souls of us two

wake up and snap out of it

CASTLES AND ASSHOLES

even if my screams
were to pierce the veil of existence
nothing of torture could compare
to the rift torn into my wisdom
to be fooled by many jesters
is one life quest necessary
but to allow it to continue
with another is fucking insanity
I wear my heart on my ragged sleeve
he ate at it like a feast of spiced meat
I was a pawn conveniently placed
outside his fortress and pearly gates
he sleeps comfortably in his perfect castle
I'll never be his picturesque queen
but he'll always be an unruly asshole
I'm my own damn wicked queen
of my own damn bloody palace
and I don't need a king beside me
to pour survival into my chalice
I will not be kept on the side, a secret
to ensure his empire does not crumble
but if his precious queen knew
we graced their chariot
she would be far from humble
keep up your charade, my lord
and I will remain a peasant ghost
don't come running for my temple
I won't be swimming in your moat

I'M MAGIC, BITCH

I am of both water and fire
ruled by the realm of my dreams
light and dark exist within me
I am capable of magical things

I put a spell on you

In His Arms

when the dark becomes too much
and the chaos of the storm inside me
is beginning to grow unbearable
how I wish I could burrow myself deep
run and pull him to me from a dream
blanket my burdens in his arms
help me forget
make it stop
if only for a moment
calm my restless tides in his heart
my sheltered protection and warmth
close my eyes, caress me softly
and when he kisses me
he makes it stop
he makes it silent
he makes it real
he *stays*
until the sun rises
for both of us

STORMCHASER

All I wanted was for someone to chase the storms in me.
To look into my calm-before disaster eyes as if tuning
into the nightly news TV screen, alarm blaring:

"EXTREME WEATHER WARNING:
IMPENDING DESTRUCTION.
SEEK SHELTER IMMEDIATELY!"

But instead, they recognized that the only casualty
would be me. Instead, they don't stay comfortable in
their luxurious heated homes, curled up safely in their
shelter of a plush blanket, waiting for the worst to pass.
Instead, they strap on their sturdiest boots and run
against the wind at full speed with urgency towards the
center of my cyclonic activity. They ride the whirlwind
with me. They brace for impact and brave the storm,
holding on for dear life. They stay, until the thunder
ceases to crash around us. Until the clouds fade and the
dust settles. Until I open my eyes, reach out, and see
and feel the sunlight holding onto me. Until I can
breathe again.

Spiralling

hearts crumble, breath shakes
in the darkness, body aches
screaming into the void
a cracking in my voice
silent noise
overwhelming fears
where are you
my dear
where are you
I call
swimming
beneath tears
come … b a c k
please
but you don't answer
you don't
hear
I lose my light
you're not
here
still
not
here

CARRY ME

touch me
like the ocean
with serene softness
teasing tides
and in reckless
wanting waves
carry me
out to sea

UNTITLED

Dear reader:

I truly hope that you never have to experience being hurt so much by someone you love, to the point where you have to force yourself to unlove them just enough to be able to walk away and leave. It is like ripping your heart from your body while it is still beating, bloody, and raw. It is like swallowing a mouthful of dirt and rocks. It is like watching your soul sink to the bottom of the ocean, and never again coming up for air.

I Am Not

I am not, and never will be
the silent woman
the gentle, the fragile
breakable woman

I am not, and never will be
the take orders woman
the sit down, the shut up
face down, ass up woman

I am not, and never will be
the shallow woman
the jealous, the spiteful
vengeful woman

I am not, and never will be
the promiscuous woman
the unfaithful, the vulgar
derogatory woman

I am not, and never will be
the taken for granted woman
the used, the abused
victimized woman

I am, simply the woman
your mother warned you about
I am the woman
who can survive with you
and survive without

ADRIFT

tides are torrential
floating along the ocean
to vast horizons

dark creatures follow
I am no longer afraid
of what lies beneath

come what may, I trust
the sea of stars above me
leave my fate to them

PUSH

please don't let me push you away
pull me closer, make me stay
I don't ever want you to leave
my fears are worn upon my sleeve
hold me tighter, until it ends
be my lover and my best friend
I need you more than you need me
but for tonight, please
just stay with me

FOOL

if I'm a fool
for envisioning the impossible
confiscate my eyes, not my mind
because I'd rather be a dreamer
if it meant being blinded forever
just to conjure an imaginary you
by my side

THE NOISE

the noise
how do you silence it?
you don't – you can't
instead, replace it
with a harmony
a symphony
anything else
that sounds better
than the wretched screeching
of the … *nightmares* in your mind
clawing their way forward … *s c r e a m i n g*
the monsters – they're coming
in   I am
   waves   *drowning*
p u l l i n g – dragging me
the voices – it hurts – make them –
/ **stop** /
him
remember his voice
remember his arms
that chase away
the dreadful dark
close your eyes
go back to that
turn the volume up
on the light around you
until it sparks
listen
for his echoing heart

BEDROCK

I have been chewing my lips
into the bedrock of anxiety
erasing the chasms with lipstick
because these claw-like nails of mine
are far too expensive and pretty
tearing them off, biting them down
would expose the hidden ugly
scars on my flesh heal too slowly
my own body covering up
my internal insanity
yes, there are days I hate my own skin
more than I care to openly admit
others I proudly wear my rebellious kit
reasoning is, I have been convinced
the bare me is not loveable one bit
my imperfections only cause
venomous spit
more controversial trouble
resentment to bubble
so, I pick, I bite, I tear
at myself until raw
masking wounds with vanity
because ignorance
is more blissful
than embracing my flaws

UNDER THE ICE

I wish I could tell you
that I am a simple
frozen winter lake
beautiful to look at
from standing on the edge
but you know of the dangers
under the thin ice
and what happens
when you walk too far
over me
I will crack
I will pull you into me
I will drown you
and then I will melt
imploding into myself
we will both be lost forever
with the depths of my cold heart

SOMETIMES, WE BREAK

some things
are easier said than done
like pulling myself
out of a night long
b r e a k
d
o
w
n
trying to convince my mind
that these demons
haven't won

I can't be strong every day

TIDES THAT BIND

I don't know how to unlove
do not ask me to try
it is not in my nature
I cannot comply
to do so would be replacing
my veins with petrified sand
bloodstream into coarse salt
morphing my brain into dry seaweed
and splaying my heart, beached out
turning a once abundant oasis
into an abandoned desert wasteland
my love is an expanding ocean
I cannot drain myself, lessen my binds
to be closer to the shallows for you
I cannot contain my tides
I would not survive
the transition
for me
to unlove
is suicide

TEMPEST

let my extremes
be equally powerful
for I can, in all elements
summon the storm
and settle it

Defeat

I try to shed memories of you
in the tears that fall down my cheeks
it isn't long before I'm swimming in them
drowning in defeat

Venom

I wish I could tell you
that I am not harmless
but I am a rattlesnake
in a barbed wire harness
I am starved for affection
coiled into myself
hyper defensive
come too close
and expect
lethal injection
I am my own venom
and I was meant to swim
into and underneath your skin
I wish I could let you
let me in
but I cannot
I belong in a cage
I will hurt you
in my poisonous rage

JOURNEY

my darling
the depths of your mind
do not scare me
where the light
cannot reach you
I will
when you fall backwards
begin sinking further
I will follow you
through the trenches
of hell
I will journey
to the floors
of your deepest sea
I will not ascend without you
even if I must take your hand
in mine to pull you free
together
breaking the surface
I promise
we will breathe

COLD

it is the most
beautiful day outside
but inside – inside of me
there is a chaotic, restless tension
my body and mind are in crisis mode
attacking me, breaking down
repeatedly
drowning in secret panic
I am struggling to tell myself
it will get better
soon
(when?)
(how?)
and I am so cold
and I wish so badly
to feel the sunlight
under my skin
but instead
when it touches me
I shiver deeper
within

MOONLIGHT

the ocean does not beg
the shore to fall into it
nor does the shore beg
the ocean to lay upon it
they simply find their way
to each other
when the moment
is right

my safe and grounded paradise
I am the hopeful, restless waves
that long to gently approach
and settle upon you again
tonight

I am regretful of my storms
rising and falling onto your shore
I have brought lightning endless upon you
drowning and depleting, eroding into me
with every eruption of my heaviest tears
still, you are here – never giving up
always enduring with me equally
this fight

I believe we will always
be drawn together in dark and light
in storm and sanctuary, in peace and chaos
by the magic tides we have created for us
under our sun
and in our moonlight

Aqua Vitae

I have loved your soul beyond
the barriers of this existence
with every wonder treasured
beneath my immortal seas

all forms of all lifetimes
have evolved with purpose
to carry your waves always
within me

water of my life

Polluted Water

I want to be kissed with saltwater lips
not a quick, candy-coated, sugary lick
I want the roughest and weathered viking
the loudest thunder and dangerous lightning
I want a war-torn, battle-hardened gentleman
give me Poseidon, with pull-me-under hands
I want a lover and a fighter equally my crazy
to be his sinful siren and loyal first lady
I want to drown in the arms of a godly whirlpool
not to slip through fingers of shrimp-like fools
I want a companion who is not afraid of my ocean
but these fish – in these waters
are too scared of devotion

something in the water – boil it over

LUXURY

wealth does not equal perfection
poverty does not equate to misery
if I am to live a life of immortality
let my heart be rich with memory

for it is wiser to survive surrounded
by not possessions, but many loved souls
a coveted stay in a serene promised paradise
is subjective in the mortal minds of people

one does not have to live a short life
to be granted only temporary luxuries
as long as the life you live with forever
is truly content in treasured peace

a life of love is immortal in perfection
no wealth can compare
to that of affection

ATTACK

I'm
angry and
I don't know
why; stay with me
stay
with me
hold me... it's
not okay, it's okay
I'm
drowning. still
here; I'm still
here... still here... still
here
I can't
feel anything; stay
with me... come back
still
here; hold
me... I'm angry
and I don't know
why
I will
smile in the
morning; stay... until it
stops
please come
back for me
don't go; I love –
no –

DANCING IN THE RAIN

I want to cross his thoughts
nightmares and dreams
like lightning stopping time

and when I do
make landfall
I will bring him
trembling
onto his knees
electrifying his mind

I am a thunderstorm
seductive and frightening
my roar is vibrating
orgasmic and mighty

I bring the darkness
there is chaos in me
dragging him into
divinity

and when he thinks
he has survived my spark
I will make him dance
inside me
as I please

aftershocks for days

WATERFALLS

maybe he's lucky – it's for the best
that he can't see me like this
or hear the screams
that erupt
from inside
of my chest
for him
and my eyes stare
into nothingness
not once do they blink
waterfalls are crashing
stinging my cheeks
and maybe
it's for the best
he doesn't see me
this weak

SERENITY

there are still moments
before moonlight, my daughter
nestles closely into my arms
tired eyes heavy with dreams
gentle lullabies keep us warm
a lifetime's worth of worries
f a d e away

the best four words
mama, I love you
with an angel's touch
upon my face

her eyes close with a smile
as do mine
right here
is my favorite place

Overseas

for years I have leaned on his shoulder
from across a dark ocean as we grew older
over time I have looked for him in every star
there is no replacing the eyes of my beholder

patience and love have been stretched afar
yet he remains still – painted on my heart
my first love will always be my rock and my boulder
he saves me from drowning while miles apart

for years I have admired his wisdom as my guide
we shared dreams and hopes for our future life
sometimes I wish I could travel back in time
if not for my chaos, I would have been his wife

forgiveness is an art we have achieved on both sides
the past cannot be changed, our fire is still alive
distance between us should only be measured
by the emptiness in his hands before holding mine

for J.S. ~ indeedio

INTIMACY

a hand adr/ft between my thighs

breath shallow agai*N*st his with mine

our eyes mee*T* with a strike of light

beckoning him to d/ve inside

tre*M*bling fingers seek and hide

strong w*A*ves pull me under his might

bodies swimming *C*loser excites

he is anchored into m*Y* soul tonight

UNDER THE STORM

you are so close, and yet so far
the very rain that falls on my body
caressing my soft, pale skin
hammering at my sunken heart
hails from the same clouds
that have travelled
to where you are
at least we are together
under the same storm
dancing in the thunder
we both share
at least we are together
if only lightning strikes apart
creating beautiful chaos
everywhere

*and if my love were to reach you only atop
the windward clouds, I would command the skies
to rain life-giving waters upon you
I would summon the brightest rainbows to kiss you
in my name after every storm*

Too Much

I always feel things… too much

like heavenly lightning in a touch
galactic fireworks in a stare
soul-shattering screams in a hush
coursing electricity in a hair
passionate crimson in a blush
devious venom in a glare
flawless diamonds
in the rough

I see immortal secrets in mortal eyes
abandoned truth behind convenient lies
colored explosions
when love lives and hope dies
I feel everything inside

with infinite senses
I ache too much
to drown in who I am
is to exist as not enough

I always feel things… too much
opening my eyes to awaken from a dream
is akin to rising like a phoenix from the dust

Visions

sometimes I believe
that I died long ago
in a white-washed room
with lilac embroidered pillows
and the air in here is light
all around me, blinding bright
there is a window
with sheer lace trim curtains
and the sun is beyond them
I am certain
their wings fly in the breeze
but I am not – will not be – free
I am immobilized on a cloud with no other
there are faint specks of only one color
my dreams replay in circles
in the details I see purple
I always see purple

even the nightmares

WALK WITH ME

I hope you follow the ghost of my footsteps
along every path I have walked on this earth
to my ending in flames
and my winter storm birth
and I hope that your feet carry you
across the edges of my life
of my dreams
to my kingdoms I reigned queen
of my hopes and my fears
and every landmark in between
I hope you stumble on every castle of sand
I have sculpted in my strong, tired hands
and I hope you walk along my beaches
but you will never find me
my screams are speechless
I am trapped
in between the waves that lap the shores
ebbing
    flowing
leaving
    returning
I cannot be found within a linear course
I am as deep as the sea
reflecting the stars above
I am a force
I am everywhere you cannot see
you are always here, my love
let this be reason to believe
that you are never alone
walking with me

End Times

What if one day, everything suddenly stopped? Would you take one step closer towards every piece of your being; across the earth in yearning of a final goodbye? In your last seconds, would you kiss them, and hope to see their eyes – closing – with yours?

I can't count my losses on my limbs and extremities combined. Sometimes, my days are spent like a silent wind chime – *h a n g i n g* in the fog. I often make no sense, but I am trying to make sense of… this life.

I hope and I dream my realities into extremes. My world is different than yours and that's okay. It's okay to be different and to see and feel so much more, because that's what we were made for.

Our souls live and breathe heart and hope, and every beautiful, meaningful thing. So, I wish on every star and every ocean I am made of. Every ocean and every star that exists below and above – that when time does stop, there will only be love.

You Found Me Here Too

of all the fish in the sea
it was the waves of fate
that brought you to me
swimming together
against all odds
surviving the currents
at any cost
you have seen my shallows
you have felt my depths
hand in hand, we emerge
with no regrets
floating on the surface
moonlight on our skin
hold me, my love
let us dive in

THE SEAS BELOW

and if you believe that you are drowning
dive further into the depths of yourself
there is always a reason
to breathe underwater
I am here to help

do not be afraid of what lurks under the surface
the darkness can be frightening, yes, I know
but remember – these creatures adapt to survive
they evolve and find their will to glow

remove the blindfold and cemented weights
free yourself from torrents of hate
swim strongly and gather your burning stars
through the sea of the universe in your heart
open your eyes to the beauty around you
you are never drifting out too far

for both above and below
are existent in your creation
magic flows freely under your veins
do you understand now, my dear?
you are the ocean becoming stronger
with every droplet of life's pain

remind yourself gently
you have endured hurricanes
you can handle
a little rain

I Believe You Can

how can one possibly
search for the stars
of their creation
while diving into the depths
of their devastation?

how can one possibly
survive the atmosphere
of their universe
and the murky waters
of their darkest curse?

my darling, when you exist
between both worlds
both worlds exist in you
you will find that anything
is possible
there is nothing
you cannot do

you only have to start reaching
you only have to start swimming
and most importantly
believing
that you can

I believe in you

my stars

are the ocean

to those who are surviving storms
in their minds and in their hearts
endlessly searching for
the stars in the oceans
of their souls

never stop reaching
never stop swimming

•

to my daughter
the soul of my stars
and the heart of my oceans

•

to all who have loved and lost me
for in both extremes, you led me
to dive deeper into darkness
and emerge brighter beyond
the infinite starlight
of myself

thank you

all my
love
Thank you

About The Author

Leanna Hewitt (LUNAIRIS) is a self-published author from Ontario, Canada. She is an avid writer and dedicates herself to transforming her thoughts and emotions into art.

Her writing often reflects powerful personal truths and lessons in love and life. She encourages growth, no matter what has been entangled into her roots. A lover of all things magic, she is always searching for the beauty in between love and tragedy through the emotional journey of her life. She embraces the light and dark of all that exists. Expressing her immense pride in striving to be the best mother she can be for her daughter, she hopes to leave behind her story to remind her that her roots are strong, and she can overcome anything the universe gives her.

She describes her inspiration as erratic and unpredictable like her, thriving in ecstatic highs and chaotic lows. Drawing from thoughts, memories, experiences, emotions, and dreams, she has adapted a passion for sharing her story in hopes of inspiring others to keep surviving. She is an admirer of the romantic, astronomical, aquatic, artistic, wild, otherworldly, fantastic, poetic, eclectic, strange, and of course – everything purple.

Her pen name, LUNAIRIS, is a tribute to the moon and Greek Goddess Iris, Goddess of the rainbow and messenger between the earth and sky.

My Stars Are The Ocean is her third collection of poetry following *Wildflowers In Bloom* and *Dreaming In Purple*.

my stars

are the ocean

LUNAIRIS